WAKEFUL NIGHTS

Fiona Kidman, born in 1940, is a full-time writer who lives in Wellington. She is the author of twelve books, including novels, short stories, poetry, non-fiction and drama. Her novel *The Book of Secrets* won the 1988 New Zealand Book Award (Fiction section). She has held the Writer's Fellowship at Victoria University, and has been awarded the Queen Elizabeth II Literature Committee's annual Award for Achievement.

Fiona Kidman

WAKEFUL NIGHTS
Poems Selected and New

V

VINTAGE

FOR Jean Dickinson

The publisher and author gratefully acknowledge the assistance of the Literature Programme of the Queen Elizabeth II Arts Council of New Zealand.

Acknowledgements: (for new poems) *Descant, Landfall, NZ Listener, Poetry NZ,* issues 2 and 3, *Poetry Australia.*

I thank Harriet Allan and Joanna Kidman for their meticulous and constructive reading of the work.

Author's note: Some early poems have undergone minor revision. 'The First Land' is a poem based on 'The Exhibition', which was the first poem in *Honey and Bitters* and 'Looking for the Exits' (from *On the Tightrope*) was originally 'Self Poem'.

Vintage New Zealand
Random Century New Zealand Ltd
(An imprint of the Random Century Group)

18 Poland Road
Glenfield
Auckland 10
New Zealand

Associated companies, branches and
representatives throughout the world.

First published 1991
© Fiona Kidman 1991
ISBN 1 86941 137 4
Printed in Hong Kong

CONTENTS

From HONEY AND BITTERS

The First Land	1
Train Song	2
Guy Fawkes '58	3
Return to Waipu	5
Making Our Bed	7
Parsley and Forget-me-nots	8
The Baked Bean Flutters	9
The Caretaker	10
Wairarapa Sunday	12
Winter Roses	14
Car Grave	15
Over Rongotai	16
Directions	17
Melon Song	18
Awakeness	19
Night Children	20

From ON THE TIGHTROPE

Words	25
Bach in the Afternoon	26
A Businessman's Lunch	28
For a Bulldog	30
Moving Day	31
Anzac '77	32
At Okura	34
Desert Fires	35
A First Day at College	37
Pact for Mother and Teen-ager	39
The Tree House	40
The Old Place	41
A Vein of Gold	42
The Touch	44
dreams/love	45
Apple Wine	46

Roots   47
Earthquake Weather   48
The Eyes of the Angel   49
About a Marriage   50
Looking for the Exits   51

The Volcanic City — Rotorua Poems:

The Swans   52
Ford Block   54
Rotorua 8 a.m.   55
Sulphur Point   56

From GOING TO THE CHATHAMS

Song of a Decade Woman   59
Made Over   60
over seas   61
doing it badly   62
The Newsmakers   63
From a postcard   64
The Rooms   65
This breaking   67
wild yes wild   68
the funny farm motel   69
A Poem for Leigh   70
The Green Book   72
Going to the Chathams   73
Photograph   81
a day in Nelson   82
Miss Wilson at the Tramways   83
The Blue Dress   84
Amelia born in May   86
Taupo writers' school   87
The Clothesline   88
Makara Beach, Spring   89
Kennedy Park   90
A prime minister gives presents
   at a royal occasion   91
An aftermath   92

Queenslander Cottage 95
Being Friends 97
Toby's Eggs 98
Writing home 99
Scenes of the Land 100
Black Hearts 101
Bulls provide semen for breeding programmes 102
The Presence of M. at a School Reunion 103
The man who loved violets 104
Prague Spring 1 (1968) 105
Prague Spring 2 (1989) 106
A Woman Photographed 107
Carole Something Like a Lombard 108
Wakeful Nights 111
The Yellow Beak 115

FROM

HONEY AND BITTERS

The First Land

My father
built a reservoir
somewhere in the north; there
cool plump frogs and I spoke
a language that only creatures
and lonely children know.

That sacred
plot of first-owned land
was ringed with gum trees stark
skeletal white limbs clothed
in tarnished silver green ghosts
of all other trees

that have shaken before gales and
when high wind spiked branch on branch
I stood beneath and said
aloud 'if it spears me
and I die then it was meant to be.'

But when the rains came rattling
the empty water tanks
and a rime of tropical
green appeared on the cracked earth
I opened my mouth
                    and drank the rain.

Train Song

It is hard to remember parents at their loving
Shoo-sh-shoo-sh-shoo

In the austerity of wartime, the bravest front was at home
Shoo-sh-shoo-sh-shoo

And after, in milking's bleary dawns
Shoo-sh-shoo-sh-shoo

Farm hands were made for sickles and lips for whistling dogs
Shoo-sh-shoo-sh-shoo.

Still, in '43, when I was three, in a night train full of Yanks
Shoo-sh-shoo-sh-shoo

He in blue, she in best, my heavy lids spied hands
  locked fast
Shoo-sh-shoo-shoo-shoo.

Guy Fawkes '58

The stars all fell out of the sky
in a single night,
and boom, they sounded cannons too.
I'd thought till then he'd father kids for me,
for that was our inheritance
                those 'fifties years,
to plan the wedding day
                and decorate the cot,
between the rugby and the beer,
the dreamy aftermath of the game won
which carried us through the whole weekend,
Saturday night and Memories are Made of This
                on the car radio,
till Sunday tea
of piecart pigs' trotters
                and love on a blanket by the lake,
fortifying us for the long week of work,
broken only by the current ball season —
clouded in 20 yards of chiffon,
Howard Morrison just a kid,
the potted ferns
and will Don Clarke score again?
All this and no regrets.

But at season's end, always the same.
As winter turned
                so did love,
put away with the football boots and hockey sticks,
waiting for another year.
A cold wind off the lake
that fiery night he said,
                'Well see ya round sometime.'
He married, wisely and Catholicly,
                the chain store lolly counter girl.

Last count I heard,
sweet, sweet, the family numbered six.
Someone tacked the stars back in the sky;
I saw them there one night and wondered
if he saw them too, or whether it was just
                    the last thing he'd done for me.

Return to Waipu

*(and some research on Norman McLeod,
a travelling Presbyterian minister)*

One stark cabbage tree, fifteen hundred
above sea level, black
mists and driving rain, then
the long run down from the top of Brynderwyn
to the flat plains of the Braigh.
I rode into town on a Road Services bus,
Like the heroine of some Western movie,
The unknown stranger, who yet knew all.

In the pub that night, some remembered me,
Though others (the Puritan past amongst the swill)
Thought I was a cheap chick
Looking for a fast small town buck.
I blundered two days round the edge of forgotten
                    faces,
Contesting the urge to remain anonymous
From heavy farm wives whose school days I'd shared.

I took the long white road to the cemetery.
What else to research but 'the Man' himself?
I found him there at last, with
the help of the grave digger —
the locals called him Clark Gable —
he lived in the salt-laden air
in a shack surrounded by a profitable collection
                    of bottles
and rags, on the same sea-front

where I'd drunk brown bomber
with the best of them, and said
farewells, in sun-honey days,
to my childhood. (Though I didn't believe it then.)
The tombstone stood in a tent of paspalum; and rust,

corrosive as his heaven and hell, tilted the palings
                    to a crazy degree.
I saw three other graves too. Friends
from the valley; one was a fair-haired child when
                    I saw him last.
I could almost believe I'd returned.

Making Our Bed

(for Ian)

Call me not beautiful when you study my form
For knowing you, I know you merely flatter
But when you hold me darkly amongst this crumpled linen
Call me beautiful if you will.

Call me not beautiful when you hear my voice
For my voice does not always please and my words are
    often cruel
But, inhabiting this pre-cut furniture (the pact was mutual)
where I am voiceless in the void
Call me beautiful if you will.

Call me not beautiful when you count the years we've had
For adders have slipped through the undergrowth too often.
Our consensus is the future. (My hand's safe in yours; alone
I'm a moth on the windowpane.)
So call me beautiful if you dare.

Parsley and Forget-me-nots

Parsley and forget-me-nots
sitting side by side
in my wilderness of fern and gorse
are all I have to grow
in my garden row.

I never grew parsley before. The coarse
rude women
warned pregnancy if they gave it me,
and I never had a handy cent to salve
their superstitious consciences.

Having borne, without success,
many children who
escaped through some faulty tube or valve;
and loved as women do

Parsley, I suppose, is for my have-nots,
And the rest is all forget-me-nots.

The Baked Bean Flutters

I'm encased between the kitchen walls,
while all the house is sleeping still:
Trim and neat, my house is full of other people's dreaming.
Piles of ironing, flat and folded,
are testimony to my day's endeavours.
Black pits outside hold only silence,
or wait! a murmur in the void?

Yes, the echoes of a quarrel
that hasn't faltered for three and forty years
over to my right, and to the left
the chuckle of love just one hour born.

Except, wait a moment, a speck of dust
goes jiggety-jig on the spotless floor,
and the kitchen-tidy groans from the weight
of its oppressions.

I'll sup a night-cap, read other people's poetry,
and deal a memory or two.
Not much left there, but the obscurantist vision
of letters folded as neatly as the washing,
yr footstep at the door,
yr 'Come, m'baby, come'
sweet against my ear.
So shall I slap a jiggety-jig
upon the kitchen table?
Maybe not. I'm afraid to turn on the stereo
and, instead, I think I'll have me
a monstrous, midnight baked bean flutter.

The Caretaker

(for Jim Gates)

He took care of his family in a tumbling house
slung with crumbling verandahs, and he talked of crops

in a fair facsimile of farmers' talk,
as he sheltered the land which in turn sheltered him,

guarding it with much hope and less skill,
for a family who would mostly disclaim that heritage.

With stumpy fag and pitted face, he drove his tractor
at the ungiving hills, and in the evening light

painted pictures and talked of many things,
and what the stars meant to him.

He called me, an only child, his other one,
casually adding me to his brood of five.

The last time I saw him, in the city long after,
(Only last year it was) he visited me, officially now

a caretaker at the country school where
I'd first known him as a girl;

doubling his time as the art teacher there, and still
instructing kids on the stars, so he said,

while ostensibly attending the rose bushes there,
and smiled his old sly smile.

Down for a conference on theosophy he was, his new
    delight,
though careless of disciples offering wheat germ and nuts

at the end of a night-long train journey
discussing philosophy with students who called him dad;

he ate heartily of a steak, drank much red wine, sang lustily
all the way to the temple door, and left me with a blessing.

Jimmy, old friend, and rock,
may your gods take care of you.

Wairarapa Sunday

Take the navy serration of the hill,
and the fluttering breath of fog
in the fluted valleys, on winter's chill
spare day.

In the field the sheep are scattered like hail,
this pale dun landscape with small
quaint cottages we've driven miles to find, for sale,
near trees

whose scribble branches wait for spring,
scratch barren messages across the sky.
But a man, a child, a girl and I
are here.

Man, mine, zippers sky with a toy machine,
he does not mark the air;
o loves, hear my voice keen
like winds from valley breath —

I will say,
etch your own patterns across this day
and dwell within the houses
of the heart,

and one may stay, and others start
without me when we leave,
for each journey's another step.

We could but die
and blood through grass would seep
as bones in earth would lie,

No more changed this landscape
than if we had never been.

It is enough, enough I give,
that in this moment that we live,

we are.

Winter Roses

I still have your mother's introduction
to you, written from an Auckland hospital
for the supposedly mad.

From our brief acquaintance I can barely recall
the colour of your eyes; more the shape
of your hands and our conversations

about the fruit of japonica, children,
and a passing reference to a private sorrow;
I know more of you through others' grief,

Yet it is neither through chance
nor second-hand pity
that I am grieving with them.

Truly, you have melted, as the frost on the vine,
or the morning star when the sun strikes;
Not for you, the burning midday heat.

Rachel, I have only some winter roses,
bought from a flower factory,
to lay beside the wounded earth.

I would have gathered flowers from the fields,
but you have chosen to leave at this harsh time
of year, when there are only bare branches

scratching at the window panes. I watched
them yesterday at your house, stripped
like our own suddenly too fragile lives.

Car Grave

The Sun God dwells near here,
gushing and spilling
a million light points
across the gussets
of the land, lining
the tucks of the bay
with the molten taffeta
of a young girl's dress.

Seven miles a man
may see to the edge
of the horizon.
That razor slick
that divides the world
is lost in glitter;
Small winds stir aerial masts.
How far from their spires

the basin of the earth?
Beneath the sharp cliffs
at our feet, lie corroded
hulks of the 'forties
Chevvy dreams, stripped naked
like a young boy's heart.
Youth chooses easy death
for symbols of its strength.

Over Rongotai

Emeralds
marigolds
cobaltic
shirley
poppies
Night lights slink across the window pane.
Precision approach
You're
on the glide ...
glide ...
glide ...
path now.
Lights stumble through the fog.
Better watching here than sharing takeoff;
Familiar
tears
blind eyes
perfunctory
goodbye
as you're gobbled off the tarmac.
I hope the radar works at every stop.
Morning
and the grey
uncompromise.
Tidy perennials, neatly planted
on a bank read 'Wellington Airport'.
Perversely
pleased to see
a reckless scatter of wild flowers
proclaiming an innocence of parallels and lines
on the bank below,
surviving
though
the lights
are out.

Directions

A bleak rain scurries across the airport
from which you are leaving.
I watch from the hillside,
having made my farewells
with small pretenses that they do not matter.
We've had few words of love,
though I've often listened to your heart's murmur
in a small white cell
where the light was always on;
defended you from your own deprecations
of an ageing body,
and heard the rattling cough
that heralds the smoker's aftermath of love.

I have no more to offer
you who still seeks answers
I do not know, having
made my own discoveries
on a different shore.
That fork in the road is not so clearly defined
as some would have it,
for along the way a myriad of tracks
branch into the bush,
and at each one's end
lies a different flower, a different leaf,
a different slope from that of the rock
where the waterfall leaps,
— and separate changes in the patterns of light.

Melon Song

black hole in the sun descending
your shoulder;
spitting and drooling words I didn't

mean to say;
ripe round melon disappearing
above me;

with a clean and telling blow
the axe bites,
pips fly from the fruit's exploding heart

Awakeness

Being of an orderly turn
she collected the various trash their afternoon had spawned;
Gathering up phrases like:

'I don't usually do this kind of thing.'
And: 'Neither do I, not really,
But you mustn't be ashamed,'

With other garbage
Not worthy of the kind of people they claimed to be.
Collecting it up

she put it in the rubbish tin
Along with the beer bottles and paper bags
they'd eaten lunch from.

It was difficult
To erase the prickle of eyes behind windows
Which winked across the sunlit day at hers;

Or a cobweb on the ceiling
she'd never seen before. But like the rest
They were tidied away.

It was only that night,
Much in need of sleep, she noticed long black strands
    of hair
On a pillow that should have been bare.

Then hands clawed thighs, dragged them apart,
And skeleton dreams invaded the dark.
Searching the house for synthetic sleep,
she stumbled on other mess

he'd left behind.
Hadn't he reminded her
That she was rather less than young?

Night Children

Capitalising on a chance acquaintance,
Her only older friend,
I heard her voice, full of fear and hesitance

late at night whispering
through my phone that the end
of her pregnancy might also be the end of her;

Then after a punishing run across town,
snapping gear changes at the lights,
we found her clutching teddy, high as fairy down.

Bitter sweet and aromatic
the smell of a joint, and fried bacon, bites
the air on the ancient stairs

as we ascend (an architectural dream to sketch,
the inside's as grotty as they come).
Despite her protests we fetch

her lover, and then she's glad for what we've done
and consents to hospital though it's not her custom
to go where authority and uniforms prevail.

As catalysts we have done what we have done,
and now we're needed no more
as hand in hand, these children of the neon sun

wander awkwardly to his car, past Western Park Tavern
and the pretty ware
in Memsahib's; she in an old man's coat

and he in a scarecrow's garb and hose,
wondrously adorned with great gold ear-rings.
The fogbound lights pick out their fragile shadows

cast against the pavement, frail night children,
with ghostly bones like gum tree branches —
migrants, both of them, from a northe'n
town; strange plants among such alien chances.

FROM

ON THE TIGHTROPE

Words

Words are

glass sharp
ice cold
slivers
of torn steel

                    on a dark street
           late at night

bamboo
under
fingernails
water
torture

                  in quiet rooms
           through all the houses

tongues
of fire
eating
bones to ash
Christ's crosses

                  in amphitheatres
           at the midday sun

Bach in the Afternoon

We play Bach in the afternoon,
it's Saturday, between movements, there
are small sounds under the eaves,
there are wild sounds in the room,

this room with a view; it takes
the smallest movement of the eye to look across
the white stirruped strait, as far as vision
will distance; as small an inflection

to look into the heart of a tree (we are
above the trees) where buds wait tightly,
looking to an early release in a storm
dark spring, as men wait,

with smaller views and larger hopes
in dull-dun green Mt Crawford prison
across the bay from where I sit;
I look down with studied care, avoiding

the larger element, there are birds like flying
dust, pecking children's discarded crusts,
the letter-box stands sentinel to my daily
concerns — my mother's unspoken prayers

that I might have a happy life, letters
from a dying aunt whose cooking smell is still
captured in an ancient cake tin, invocations
from my father, dental appointments

and the larger insurrections of contracts,
deadlines and other grails which beleaguer
my writer's life; I look and look into this
tiny space, blades of grass, leaves, sparrows

dead branches, the rejected food, the white box,
sounds accumulate around me, and I fight to resist,
how I fight, but yet I raise my eyes,
there's no escape, the world pours in, I am blinded.

A Businessman's Lunch

While sitting in a restaurant, ready to close,
he told her how many books he'd written and how many
more copies than hers they'd sold,
he described with a flourish, between garlic
and dandruff, what a fabulous lay he was sure she would be,
and then recoiled —
his skin crawling like a snake through grass
like a snail retreating into its shell
or a wet sea anemone sensing danger —
when she touched his hand
(she could have sworn his penis turned inside out on the
    spot).

The subject of children and wives
was thoroughly aired ('I get plenty of high class sex
at home,' he murmured, 'it's our minds which will enrich
this entire situation,' and then
proceeded to demolish the myth
of minds in the feminine gender.)
Children, well of course, he had four,
and that, you know, meant a lot of love,
as if twice as many children as she,
ensured twice as much love, or worse,
that possession was nine points of the law
and hers simply didn't exist at all.

They discussed the black hole
in the mattress through which they
both claimed to fall
when the nights were dark,
but when she erred, by expressing an opinion,
she suddenly saw his mattress, under a paranoiac quilt,
and knew that it would always be separate
beds for them:
she didn't need to wait for nightfall

to know that her dark still had room
for stars, and a crimson moon
rising between her knees.

For a Bulldog

If our dog could write his autobiography,
his early life must surely be a harrowing story
of deprivation; think how he was severed
not only from the umbilical cord at birth,
but soon his tail as well.
Poor fellow, bound over in slavery to a vicious
master, who educated him in ways
of corruption, till recently still suffered
the swift kick to the solar plexus while breaking
the ribs of cats and attacking other dogs (and not
even a true fighting spirit at that).
His squashed face tells a lonely tale,
shunned he wistfully looks at children
who scream in terror when they see him,
or worse, laugh and point.
When he came to live with us, we had him
psycho-analysed, he's been through
transactional analysis, made many profound
decisions, accepted moral values; now he's
settled for being a loner, except for us,
gave up sex — although he occasionally
propositions me;
he's settled in a rut, is grateful for his food,
and if he has a vice, it's killing bees
amongst the marigolds, the stampede through
the African Giants is heavy on drowsy summer
afternoons. But *c'est la vie*,
old men count flies on walls, suck their soup,
and have erections in public places;
after all this is my dog's story, not theirs.

Moving Day

(for Dave and Yvonne)

Today we have moved to our castle
among the patches of flowering broom;
There were buttercups on the window sills
and wine glasses on the ledges,
A choir of bees, an orchestra in the stream,
and a fiery furnace in the sunlit sky.

So we have come at last to this place
to dwell between the invisible walls,
Where you will let me pass
from time to time,
But never stay my return
Or pull the drawbridge up.

Here between the hours of twelve and two
we'll talk about democracy and humanity,
and our responsibility to others,
But at the final hour, you'll never let me go,
nor will there be weeping,
in the shadow of the castle walls.

Anzac '77

(a sequel to Guy Fawkes '58)

The celebrations are both of fire
and equal exercises in futility,
exploding stars or bleeding
heart poppies,

we of the grey generation
might have learnt something,
or so we would think, yet
as I said my goodbyes
nearly twenty years ago
beneath a sky of falling rockets,
how could I imagine that this morning,
with last posts tootling ghostly nonsense
everywhere, I would hear a boy's name
on the radio, killed in a brawl,
I was sure it was your son.

He could have been ours,
but that was long ago,
I bear no rancour,
love has honed many a sharp new edge
since then, and right now,
all I can honestly recall
of you,
is a quiet (unseemly then) capacity
for grief.

The summer's last carnations bleed
on my window ledge. Across the years
I stretch my hands, cup them briefly,
expecting to hold your bursting heart,
and rightly for such presumption,
find them empty:

the fires rain down, each generation
determines some obscene new absurdity
to maintain its rituals.
We did no better,
and all our stars were hollow.

At Okura

Under the tree of crimson ash
at Okura
we share remembered time
baked bodies play the naked game
on the sand beside us
your face is stripped of time
to when we two knew
of no unquenchable fires
and coming joys
were still half seen
I loved you then girl
I love you now
but the ash falls
and the blue tide
relentless rides
the bay
all the way
to Whangaparaoa.

Desert Fires

I

The morning lake was ironed flat
as fresh blue linen, a heron
was wedged in a willow tree branch.
I turned away from a lover's kiss,
unwilling to plumb the heart of bliss,
for that's Pandora's box,
and I have worn memory like a shroud
too long; as with that chocolate box lake,
I cannot lift the lid,
there are evil sweetmeats
in its depths.

II

I did not know that the road south
would be so unsafe. Still
both victim and plunderer, seduction
was imminent. The hills lay like breasts,
the valleys opened like thighs, sister Sappho
joined me as I plucked each bush,
wild purple heather, downy toi-toi hair,
my hands bled from the rose bush thorns
yet still I gathered their scarlet hips,
I could feel their shape against my mouth:

III

I travelled on, the desert grew dark,
a strange cloud blotted out the world,
approaching cars warned me of the peril beyond,
with full-blown headlights at height of day:
then I saw the tongues of fire licking the plain.
Sisters, we consume and are consumed,

35

every country has its heart of darkness
and every heart its core of fear.
So I passed beyond the fires
and on the home strait run,
I told myself,
it all seems safe enough again.

A First Day at College

Only born,
I have seen your placenta slide across the sheets,
nearly killing both of us in that
premature ejaculation
of natal blood
(placenta previa I believe they called it)
heard my gutteral voice turn to animal sigh,
slow and quiet pain
upon a cloud of pethedine,
expected the worst,
yet found you, as in a miracle,
perfect.

Hate swelled in the breast
beside the clogged veins of milk,
as in the night watches
you dragged an empty nipple,
cracked and worn
from trying too hard,
viewed your eggshell skull,
darling how easily it would have broken
the cranium impaled upon the dresser;

Your father was your knight, you share
the burnished armour of his skin.
It was he who rescued you. The fever
settled and died, yet still I use him often,
shaping around him
each raw excess of mine,
each irrational outburst,
when the sky splits like atoms
and no one is safe. It is to this
that you have unwittingly,
protestingly been born,
perhaps a monstrous pity

to inflict upon you this chaos.
I understand the beginnings of your pain
reflected in my own old and many sorrows;
one cannot retrieve a birth, however singular.

I see you in the blue and teeming flood,
you have escaped my clutching frantic hands —
escape, escape my darling,
in the flow towards the hill.
Only born,
your survival has deceived me thus far,
I watch you from the road below
but you are ascending still;
small one, suddenly grown tall,
I will not call you back.

Pact for Mother and Teen-ager

Girl, we've quarrelled
in a motel in a strange town.
It's 2 a.m. and tomorrow
I'm due to drive north all day
on the holiday we've planned
this six months past.
If you were a lover,
I'd have thrown you out;
if you were your father,
I might have had a bitter-sweet
reconciliation. But as you are
my child, I watch you sleep
tangled in bedsheets and tearstains,
and try to plan the shortest way
out of town.

The Tree House

Today the tree house is surrounded by sunlight
and the neat squat branches, cropped back
to allow light on your father's garden patch
glow through dappled leaves;

Yet only last night you shouted
with apparent delight and screamed at me
to look at you, look at you
as a storm from the south

lashed up an ugly frenzy, tearing
through your hair as you nailed
up flotsam from other people's lives,
pilfered from their multi-bins.

How I feared for you, resisting my pleas
to come down, come down won't you,
as black night blotted out your shadow
above the cliff top where the ngaio stands.

Others claim to read in your mind,
things I cannot understand. I see only valour
in one who, in waking, so dares the pitface,
when sleeping holds such terrors.

The Old Place

It was a grey morning
lying idle before summer storms
when I took the three of them
to the old place, half hidden by flame
tipped hakea and blackberry thorns.
I could not have seen how cruel it would be,

though not so much to them, for
now I can see it was a self-inflicted pain (a familiar trait).
Standing close, they stared yet in distance
at the hut, climbed dutifully through bales of hay,
cameras at the ready, avoiding cracks in the floor,
their eyes asking me to tell them it was all a game.

I showed them the lean-to, now standing apart
and open to the weather, exposed in every beam;
it had been my bedroom, I explained to them
and pointed to the shelf where my books had stood
above the place where I had lain, and my young heart
had lurched its way to each unsteady dream.

That night the floods broke, and water
swirled knee-deep through camp-sites. We headed south,
headlights on, thirty all the way, in tropical rain.
I saw that room then, all awash. Maybe I do them
less than justice, but my son and daughter
have not spoken of that place again.

A Vein of Gold

This discovery was beside a Grecian sea,
or so I imagine it, for you had seen
a dozen seas, and I not one of them, only this:
it was evening, realms of fire
sprung from the caps of the waves.

You'd a large suitcase in the car,
you were shy about its battered shape,
explained that your uncle gave it to you
when you were nine
for visits to the seaside.
'Well we've had a trip to the seaside,'
I said, as if it were of no consequence,
this meeting. Perhaps
it was not.

But you kissed me.
But I was trapped.
But there was gold dust in my eyes, it
spread over everything, and through
your hair and on
your skin.

Remembering this, I know however sharp and hard
the heart may turn for things which end before
they begin, and however the flesh may break
under glancing touches which turn to blows
in memorial nights, when the bedclothes are sand,
and the dark is the tide, and silent cries
are the thunder of encroaching waves which
eat bones to bleach-white fragments of driftwood,
to cast them up on beaches far away;
                    there is all that,
yet still there is that one last wild gesture
of the arm flung high; take that arm before

the waters close, drive the needle deep, there
at last in mine, you will find, there was one
pure vein of gold.

The Touch

When I wake in the dark fur of the night
and I'm alone, I press my face
against the night's fur as if it were
your chest, that I might more easily
return to sleep.

When I wake alone, on a wet morning
with the rain pounding like blood
on the windows, then I open my mouth
and your tongue on mine is rain,
and blood, in my mouth.

dreams/love

I cup my hands
round winter stars
they slide through my fingers
like mercury
plummeting deep
beneath an icy sea
to lie in jewelled spires
cold fires
glittering
beyond my grasp

Apple Wine

(for Sam)

Young Hunt's
brought good
apple wine
in a fat
flagon; he's
full of love
and riches,
gorged with
his success
at stud, a son
full of warmth
and his mother's
good dapple
breast; apple
wine, apple
wine, apple
bloom my own
children flower
from buds
opening full,
how rich
the ripening
fruit, apple
wine, apple wine,
the rich scent
filters from our
children's petal
skins; how strong,
how lovely
the trees. Friend
let us drink
wine together,
and remark on
the growth of those
which we tend.

Roots

We met on some pretext, you
emphatically chauvinistic about paying
for food we had difficulty
in eating, said 'leesure' for

leisure, in order to impress
me with your cosmopolitan
outlook; I made my too familiar
joke about all my overseas

experience being confined
to the Picton Ferry. It was
the truth about both of us
and infinitely less.

I am reminded that under
green foliage, roots lie in the dark,
tangled and matted, undisturbed
unless some fool should break the sod,

and I know too that one
long tap root can break open rock.
You are leaving, and it's as well
for we cannot bridge the years

with words, yet I am afraid
to touch you. School days
cannot be resurrected from dusty classrooms:
our common pasts lie best in darkness,

and we were wise to pretend, with small
half-smiles, that they did not matter,
that we had come for some other reason,
though what it was, I've already forgotten.

Earthquake Weather

For three days now, the air
has been quiet and still.
Yesterday, a vase walked across
the mantelpiece. A friend and I
have traced the fault line
along a map. It is very close.
There is neither sun, nor yet rain,
and the wind has departed too.
The crickets have stopped singing
and the children's quarrels grown bitter.
We wait, sealed in this
grey vacuum.

And when we went to bed
last night, the moon slanted
between the curtains (yes,
we still have a moon),
catching your white smile
in a dazzling glitter. We
who have known rage and lust,
regrets and promises, have come
to understand love. I was afraid
you were about to devour me.
I wish this weather
would break soon.

The Eyes of the Angel

There's a sepia tint pinned inside our wardrobe door,
three kids stand in a row, their drawers hang down
to their knees
against a backdrop of corrugated iron, rust
and the wind whistling by, when their father and mother
don't come home any more, any more
and the man on the railroad track
takes mummy away, singing, singing
and daddy goes away, crying, crying
to the sanitorium black;
the tussock lies flat on the wind
and the echoes of the train hurry on down, o father
be slow, and lover be quick
the swift grasses bend and the night wind is sad
and the walls remember the sounds
and the images grow on the edge of the world;

I married a man but never knew
the place from where he'd come.
This I do know: when his father died, mother came back
and she walked, she walked down the funeral track, the track
where they carried that coffin on high
and a stone angel on a grave raised her trumpet
and blew high noon, as we walked on back
saying father and mother, where
did you go, all those years ago
when the train whistled by the lonely shack?

But there are no days of reckoning,
and that woman was wise
to regard me then with eyes
like those of the angel in stone.

About a Marriage

We are empty now, like husks
    of corn when the yellow
    cob has been devoured;
Like shells on a white beach,
    hosts who have returned
    their guests to the sea.

We have gouged each others' eyes
    and eaten them like cannibals,
    our limbs are bleeding and broken,
mutilated, as in car crashes,
    and other, and various nightmares.

Yet still we come again and again,
    crawling on hands and knees
    across the bloody battlefield,
    watching out for landmines all the way,
    and you restore my sight,
    and I bind your wounds,
    and we are ready to make love
        again in the night.

      Hush love,
    summer will come again
    to ripen the ears of corn
    and flood tides
      bear new gifts.
      Only come quickly
    to gather them,
for the harvest cannot wait.

Looking for the Exits

I was with friends in a cafe
and I lost myself.
I ran out into the night
to find myself, and they followed me,
not understanding the agony
of this particular loss.
Cruel, I sent them away and went to a place
overlooking the sea,
to howl at the moon.

Nights later, I returned to that same point
still expecting to find what I had misplaced.
Dark came suddenly —
in an over-crowded city,
in a place I thought I knew well,
I took a strange turn
to a no-exit street
crowded with trees
and a lack of any single person or house.

The dark hardened.
Rain fell.
I turned inwards. I rediscovered
what all the time I had been trying to lose.
I reject self:
I cannot escape it,
or grief for my friends.

THE VOLCANIC CITY –
ROTORUA POEMS

The Swans

The black swans demand
that I should write about them:
for years they have haunted me,
since that frosty morning long ago
when my child and I sat waiting
beside Lake Rotorua.
We could hardly see the water
for the vapour that lies over
that place in winter,
a condensation I suppose,
of lake mist and sulphur
fumes; there was no colour
there, except orange peel
lying in a trail like Indian
beads on the ground:
then I saw the black swans,
they came out of the water
and surrounded the boy,
hissing with death rattles
in their arched throats
and their wings were lifted like capes.
I would have killed them if I could;
predator and victim are much alike,
the cycle goes on:

Now, in another town, I see Greek widows
in black weeds sail eternally
through city streets.

They are like the swans,
hunted, and hunting,
for their children.

Ford Block

I knew the lady the land was named for,
she was rich and superior,
I've no reason to believe she intended
her namesake to be poor and inferior,
but that's what it is,
how the children play

The Jokers and the Wreckers are away
at their deadly game
in stolen cars, chicken with variations
under Ngongotaha's long dark shadow,
the mountain where the patu-paiarehe stray,
we'll gladly take the blame,
the children say as they play,

if borstal relieved the boredom,
there's nothing to do, and it's quiet and it's cold,
we don't want to grow old, what's the point,
we'd rather be bold for a night,
our mothers and fathers supply the cheap labour
for the tourist trade, and the fat cats' larder,
the children weep as they play

you can put us behind bars
but give us a frost under the stars
before you do, we cannot unlock the gates
where our parents scrape the plates, we're foul
and disgusting and evil,
but down Ford Block way

that's how they've taught us children to play
us children to play
us children to play.

Rotorua 8 a.m.

We lift over sleeping morning houses;
I could pluck my mother from
the tarmac, her diminishing
is more than the encapsulation
of all our days;

I could lift with one hand
the roofs of houses, as a child
would a doll's house cover,
and beneath the lids see
your sleeping forms.

It's a water colour morning
broken too early, a Sunday,
and at that, the first round
of daylight saving, the plane's half-
empty, the travellers have forgotten
                              to rise.

I see through these several trans-
parencies, my own face awash and
puffy blue; I have dreamed dreams
all night, and woken in fear that
they be not true.

Now as I command the world
from giant's height, I know that dreams
do not lie. Not distance, not size,
not time, not tears, can keep me here.
I'm afraid, yet still I'm heading home.

Sulphur Point

Sulphur blooms across the point
like Cape daisies,
seagulls conduct a blitzkreig
on garbage,
spent condoms litter rocks,
bleached skeletons
pose as trees,

while I,
helpless,
am frozen on the tightrope
between
then and
now

regardless
a ceramic sky spills inexhaustible
white
light.

FROM

GOING TO THE CHATHAMS

Song of a Decade Woman

(towards midnight 31.12.79)

The flickering blue shades of the screen
are drawn. We're done
with all those pictures.

Let's try music then: xylophones play
Jesu Joy of Man's Desiring and the pipes
of Pan rust like us.
That's enough: they bid the hour.

The storms have destroyed our garden
this year. Earlier this evening
I replaced the plants; a late flowering
can still be hoped for (born '40,
turning 40). The children
send greetings from afar, that's how
          we thought
it might be but could not entirely believe
          it would be so.

Ten years ago we didn't know
anyone who'd died, now we seem
to be almost the only ones left alive;
this morning I began to bleed,
in ten years that will be done
          with too;
tempered, steeled, bloodless,
will some blood
still rush to our heads?

Made Over

My seams are fragile
tear easily in the bedclothes.
Breasts snag like broken toenails
on loose threads; head blanketed
against you

I dream   clear air
curled fingers unprising you:
find empty space
break patterns.   Patches
and mends: holding fast.

over seas

yr poems
pursue
me across many seas
yr face remembered
in a glass chalk
white mouth
a misshapen
O
(primaeval prime evil)
hair green
streamers powdery
skin stretching
at the seams
extraordinary
that you so protect
the vulva keep
passion
intact i
of course
am you

doing it badly

i'm flashing
myself, throwing
up my skirts
above my pants
like an old whore
on party night,
showing blood
to the moon;
i am ready
to let it leak
down my legs
plunge my fingers
in this sticky
coagulation
touch it to my mouth
and cover my face

with scarlet juice
like dahlia stains
look i've had all
these years
of screaming and cry-
ing and hurting
and behaving badly
being inappropriate
and trying to hide the pain
and disguise the smell
i've had enough
of this bloody
thirty year flowering

before it's finished
can't i just show
you
my guts?

The Newsmakers

for Fay Weldon

On the blue screen
the woman from overseas
looks round and warm and earthy.
Her looks are deceptive. I think
she is saying one thing and meaning
another.
So do I, but then I
am tense and frail and sleepless
from a night of too many words.
Let us talk of husbands, says the interviewer,
in our small chat beforehand. The woman
laughs. Mine is twelve thousand miles away,
she says. I can say anything
I like. Can't I?

I say nothing. There is nothing
to say. I know
I will smile
and get it right.

My father taught me
to collect birds' eggs and blow
their yolks into a bowl,
to cradle the outer shells
on cottonwool, so that we could view
the colours
through glass. I place myself
in the chair, drain the centre,
expose the shell. The cameras
roll. See
how hard
I am.

From a postcard

you say that you are both very happy
and very unhappy
as you gaze at spires and temples
and behave like a tourist;

it is more than distance that separates
the heart, the sharp decline
of time suggests that deliverance
is past. There is pleasure

here in buds shattering before the spring
advance, the turning and banking
of earth, for the new season's garden. But
the winds blow fierce here

and the flowering is an annual affair.
I know better than you
that this little indian
summer will pass; we will have

as ever, the ritual uprooting
for the autumn fires.

The Rooms

When I walk
into a hired room
in some strange town,
I do not know what I will find except
for some established certainties: a shower
(sometimes a shower cap, per courtesy
of the management), cubes of soap,
a sleek kettle, discreet colour scheme,
and a pushbutton radio
to keep company with the wakeful nights,
         and yes, a well-stocked liquor
cabinet if I'm going expense
account:
         I can afford
a certain irony, for it's
me that counts in there.
         Nothing else. No one.
I can move the pain
across the board, divide the costs
and take respite from you, and you,
and you. It's only the stranger lurking
in the mirrors
that catches me unawares.
                  And when I leave

the room of the motor hotel
punctual at 10 a.m. checkout time,
they (my impersonal slaves
for a day) will wipe away
my fingerprints from the formica,
erase my body odour,
clean the lavatory seat,
and change the linen. There will
be no more imprint
of me. The heart and bottle

may be empty: my head
will be full
of clean spaces. Nobody
will catch
up with me.

This breaking

for my son, Giles

It's so long since I thought
my heart was breaking;
all the men I know
have grown scars on dreams
or come to terms

with my impatience.
Yet now there's you, wild young animal
emerging out of bad nights, and the tree house
                                    jungle,
descended into the streets, stalking alone
in that despair, like the breaking light
that heralds dawn, the boy

breaking into man. At your
insistence I watch from afar, fear
for the hard concealing tissue
which seals away hearts,
                    hope you can be
the kind of man

who'll come to terms with something,
yourself, and women like me, know
either way, we both bend —
come close to breaking
at this bitter loving
half-way point.

wild yes wild

my wild wild one
in the neat black dress
and the dark
dark dream upon your face;
I think of ruth
and i think of sappho
and i do not know
the way between
o my daughter o
my daughter thinking of you
the singer sings the song
and i know no other song
than the curve
of your high
cheekbone to the matching
thigh. i offer you
coke and camembert
and a week off your rent
and the wild wild
dream that you'll
be free

the funny farm motel

in the yellow-on-the-grass
morning light
your hands, your
good hands, thick
and spiked
with hair
turning the bacon
turning the bacon over
in the pan and mating
it with the eggs
at the funny
farm motel with
        its:

                    arabian nights
                    room with gold
                    tassels, springtime number
                    with the wooden bananas on
                    the drawers, and the farm-
                    yard unit with the red
                    rails around the king-size
                    bed

    and afterwards
scones by the sea
and the straight rain
falling on the sun
        umbrellas,
talking about
blue movies
and your slow smile
never breaking into
laughter
as we recalled
the funny
funny farm motel

A Poem for Leigh

In the space of one window frame
there is solid green
and then, on closer inspection, green again
many times; jasmine
shooting early,
ginger
plants rampant
from a summer that hardly
                    happened;

a dead ponga, and other
native plants
I should have learned
to name: I hold a dead pen
unable too, to write your name
and hunt
in vain for wild nasturtiums
on the bank, a sharp citric shine
amongst that many layered green,
as I still hunt
for your bright head
on unlikely corners of city streets:

                    your hair,
is it really growing
still? that wild mane
of gold lying
in wait for a false spring
and another summer
that will not come?
has no one told you
deep down there
that the ice age comes
and that you wait in vain —

or does your own wild gold still
        light the lights
sister?

Night comes,
I've no more time to look, and
dark has closed the window.
I break eggs in the pan,
watch it fill with yellow
see the yolks, how, they froth and heave,
make food
that we'll devour, and remember
that blood
blossoms too.

The Green Book

for Sharon

I carry a bound green book
with blank pages to record
things that matter.

I press wild flowers
from river banks, they bubble
the smooth paper. Today

it is light in the garden
and the warmth on my skin
that I note with such care,

and the tomatoes ripening
at last on the autumn
vine, and orange

cactus dahlias, a premature
cap of snow on the Rimutakas.
The solemn core

is warmed; only
dreams memories
sensation hold. Face lifted,

a temptation
to eye the sun.

Going to the Chathams

1

The land is dark & flat
trees bend towards the earth
this indeed a *bitter beloved*
place set in a squall-swept sea

in the bus smoke thickens we bear
towards town in dull light
puddles of white sand glisten
in shallow indentations beneath

the level of the sea which may
overtake all in a small orange
and pink chamber without
locks writing on my typewriter

if I may not say I love
you let me say from this strange
and distant place that I think
of you with gentle heart

2

on the wardrobe   six unopened
books   in the wardrobe
pink doughy flesh   a tin of lambs'
tongues in aspic   1.125 litres
of Scotch   & a packet of biscuits
in case of missing
dinner   & other emergencies

3

*... the Land Settlement Committee on the
Chathams will insist that both the applicant and his
or her spouse must be able to settle in happily among
the island community, and cope with the sometimes
unusual conditions on the Chathams ...*
(newspaper, 23.9.82)

Good day beau how you
going beau a whole race
has died here lament
the Moriori the crayfish
boom has been and gone
the gamblers and the whores
the fast buck and the sharp
dealers
    this was a cauldron 10, 15
years back the worst
Pacific hell since
Kororareka the pits man
the pits   in a curious
migration of the sea the crayfish have moved on   the islands
returned to sleep
      the Ministry says
some day the fish may
return beau how you going
      beau?

4

The old house where belladonna
lilies grow outside
is full of antiques failing
at the seams: a gramophone
dressers decorated with leadlights
a rusting piano & the north

74

westerly curling the edges
of the diseased wallpaper
over the matchboard lining
where the Chatham rats
nest. I hear them, move quickly
from a shape in the gloom.

5

At Owenga

the schoolmistress
in the woollen cardigan
sits on the beach
with her eyes riveted
to the horizon
waiting for the barge
of sheep to come
from Pitt

'sometimes they come and sometimes
they don't,' she says.
it's saturday. she can wait
all day, or all weekend
if she wants
till the children
come again.

6

smoke gets in your
          well wouldn't you
just know   the eyes have
it (hard & blue)   and if it's not the weed
that's blinding the mist over
the bay obscures
the fishing boats   sidling
at anchor   & the moon pushing

its way   into the sky   with such
luminosity   coming out
of the clouds   it's saturday night
& i'm not lonely
            caught on a stranger's glance

7

some things go
                on forever
                an accumulation of stars
the past which just keeps   growing longer
Time magazine said
in a chopper over 'Nam
                the CIA agent
was shot   through the head
                alas poor Rembrandt
I knew him
                briefly
working a newshen stint
the week LBJ   turned it all in
& the big boys   (like top brass
that ran the world   mind fuckers
                in gilt-edged hats)
shook   ashen faced   clustered
in a hotel room   certain
                they were out of jobs
jesus one moment
in history   some things do change
the world
                mine not theirs
the carnival had just BEGUN
later   much though it seems
like yesterday (things run into each other)
Germaine Greer   saying (it)
(G.G. where did you *go*?)
now that blew it all open then
pouring down Lambton Quay   first demo ever
yeah   a late developer if you like

& if you're looking
for the one perfect
fuck   the lady's   not for burning
over the sea
there's one light
glowing   in the dark
if you walk down the beach
                    towards it
it moves further away   if you turn
& come back   (and the temptation is there
just to keep
          walking
            on into the night)
there are 10 or 20   lights hovering in
the township of Waitangi
this is the first place in the world
where the sun rises   you might as well say
where the edge of the world   begins
which is a sobering   thought the division
of east   from west
in much the same way
that the Columbia
Bank divides   the Tasman
from the Pacific   only the scale
of this is so
          monumentally
much greater   in a 6'x10'
unlocked cell   perfection
is yes yes
within   without love &
the sea & everything going on & on
or at least until morning
the distance between rocks & the stars
is so far

8

crayfish stew for Sunday
breakfast   dressed neatly appear

refreshed at Saint Augustine's church
of memorials for the sea's dead

9

*The Chatham lily; a small tolerant plant; it has pink
or blue flowers in the spring. It used to cover the
islands. Now it is rare.*

The pain of women begins early here
love is a relative matter
tenderness nearly extinct   like the lily
the lily is near enough to dead
the covenant of salt is over
Saint Augustine hear our prayer

10

When Father Frank preached
against the tour they fired
warning shots to scare him off
men from the Canterbury Plains
snigger in the bar at night
when the *smokeys* are asked
to leave but those dark locals
hear only what they want & if
this priest was foolish enough
                    to rattle
sticks on the iron roof
when the 'boks Test match was playing
on the radio
all that was missing was the
                    bloodshed
& they were happy to let
him have that too if that's the way
he wanted it. yes the mainland
is 800 kms away
& mainlanders from the north
whisper

when they say
A BRAVE MAN FATHER FRANK

11

At the Basalt Columns

Elizabeth would say write down everything
you know about rock formations Kidman
Harlow would remark on an affinity
with buildings as if a hole in the rock
might present itself as shelter
Sharon would ask what they'd had for lunch

Basalt: a type of volcanic rock very rich in iron ...
basalt lava erupted on the surface usually flows
very readily — often with almost stream-like rapidity

researched not known large parts
of New Zealand are still in the process
of being pushed up out
of the sea land masses the ice age
not much else friend the existence
of faultlines & fossils of course

as to you yes admittedly a swift vision
of temples & you I'd tell
                that it was home-baked
bread & paua fritters taken with
the visiting cloth that I enjoyed
the black flesh more than I thought
possible but that was the way

of things here fear is a constant
factor the tsunami (they call it 'tidal
wave') has come often enough a football
team less one man vanished on a calm
unspectacular day sailing from Kaingaroa
to Waitangi no bodies no wreckage perhaps

some deep gravitational pull downwards
the sullen edge of prevailing violence
locked in the sea the sea beating against
the Columns the clenched lava frozen
above the spray watching back to the land
for a long time (she would seek a stranger's face)

12

On Te Whaanga lagoon's flatbed
the teeth of shark 55 million
years old wash towards my gum-
booted feet long pale blues

excellent specimens or dark & sharp
like fragments of fired bone snagging
against the fluted shore wind
whipping over this long drawn-out

extraction from the shallow surge
beyond the swans with white
underwings raised over the banks
of flounder here on the beach

they call Blind Jim it's easy
to believe no people exist
the ancient porcelain of the sky
envelops the wasteland a chance

the Bristol will not retrieve me
but cold bites hard at the ankle
& these harsh these beautiful islands
are for leaving I pack the old fangs

in the pocket of my jeans   listen
already for the morning plane await
lift-off   newspapers   time
mattering   & believable acts again

Photograph

So it comes to this that
one day you will wake
& you will no longer be young
age will have bitten   your throat
will puff like a pigeon's
in your passport photograph

leading to a closer examination
the acquisition of a crepe-
like tissue in the crook
of your arm will become apparent
it will be clear that
                    the morning ache

cannot be attributed to a virus
this time the flutter in the eyelid
is not a reminder of an excellent
night about town rather that vanity
persuaded you to abandon
your glasses when you needed

them most you would think
it was enough to undo you
like knitting dropped
off the needles an irretrievable loss
but it's a long yarn if you keep holding onto the end & picking up here
                    & there

a day in Nelson

one of Jill's 5 cats turns somersaults
on the bough of a willow pattern tree
tilting towards the lemon coloured

sea George has a 3 wheel bicycle
to ride along the street & shelves
designed within his reach & grows
vegetables profuse as flowers in the park

Rachel writes & wins prizes (4 today)
& some of us sit in the sun drinking
& talking easily about plane crashes

Miss Wilson at the Tramways

The newspapers report that Miss Wilson who visited
the Tramways Hotel last Sunday night had a pixie-
like face and long brown hair.

She was the only guest
at the rancid old inn. What did
Miss Wilson do between the hours of six

and one? Perhaps she sat, pale
and composed in her room, her hands
folded in front of her, or

opened the Gideon's Bible on the dresser
as the minutes ticked past and climbed
into a bed with tight white virginal

sheets plastered to its sides. Did she have a hot
water bottle and had she brought a toothbrush?
Miss Wilson, her face to the window,

watching ... then turning to brush her long brown
hair 99 times as she gazed at her reflection
in a plain deal mirror, catching the inner

smile of a pouke, before she took the key
from her jeans pants pocket to open the door
to the underworld. Two hooded men and a crafty

catch of 14 grand, and the innkeeper trussed tight
as a colonial goose until dawn. Miss Wilson, what a ball
you had at the Tramways Hotel.

*pouke/pixie

The Blue Dress

There was me
getting off the little plane
from the north
and careless
enough with my hair
undone and wearing
jeans as if
I was one of the film moguls
riding in the little plane
with me

and then there was you
there was you love
waiting in the hum and buzz
waiting in the big terminal
in the strange city

amongst the false gods
waiting there for me
as well, only I didn't hear
them or the calls
on the speakers in the big space
because it was you love
yes you alone and brave and out

on your own
at last:
    hungry of course
and smaller
than I thought
in a spreading blue
denim maternity dress with frills
at the neck straightening
me up so I'd pass well enough
to be with you and neither

of us hearing the voices
calling me, because
I was
with you love I was
with you
in your glowing growing blue dress.

Amelia born in May

smelling of jonquils
at the wrong time
of year; at an unexpected
season when yr
unpredictable birth
seemed to have given
up on us all. 'The smell's
got to be right,' yr
grandfather sd, 'that's how
you know
     she belongs,'

remembering yr uncle Giles & the deep
scent of earth (& his digging
& turning it over with his hands
when he was older) & an
animal muskiness
the dog after its bath & ripe
brie & a sheepskin
after it's been in the rain

& now you who we call
meat chops   delicate & un-
blemished as the inside skin
of an egg & yr shit
smelling (& looking) like pumpkin
                soup
fruit & flowers   flowers fruit
& vegetables   all produce
in the ungiving month.

Taupo writer's school

for my father

At mother's house your pictures
of this place hang on the walls colours
soft as tissue the wash of the water
in the paint reflecting these

mists and oh the sky over the water
is darkening the waves on the lake
sharpen like tousled lace the hem
of my shift   the spiked

cabbage tree rears its head
above
   the edge of the window-
sill level with the heads
of my quiet students scratching

their verse it always seemed to me
that you shouldn't have put that bird
right at the forefront the rocks
are better and more difficult

to climb at evening well it's
impossible not to think of you (here) old
man now that you're dead and your
late drawings oh yes the light

on the lake the wind shifting
the tops of the waves and the night
leaning in on me   it's been
a bright day beneath the mountains

The Clothesline

for Amelia at 5 months old

Amelia the sky that amuses you
so much is 2 prs of trousers
& a nightshirt
on the clothesline
above the rooftop
the wind
makes them bigger
than dad
or the man next door who wears
them your daddy Pepe the chef in
his checked pants going to his
work is not as fat as
the man hung
on a cloud
in the wind Pepe cooks
& sings you to sleep.

Makara Beach, Spring

It's this skin of happiness that holds
me together. Like an olive round an anchovy's
body. More loosely, like Maggie's neck
collected in folds over her collar bone
sliding about, no special grip on the world.
A dog's life all right. But god, it's good, beside
the sea collecting wild flowers and weeds
of new zealand. Blue eyed daisies, white as foam
and dark as the sea's centre, the middle's
what counts, and yellow, there's yellow
flora all over the place. I've even got you
collecting the encroaching cream off
the land, and a smudge of silver edged
leaf. A heron
bows, arches, stalks across
stones. A bunch of overland cyclists stand
aside, smile. Indians picnic in the shade
of a cliff. A Vietnamese child lies down
waiting to be rescued on the round
rocks. A tide of gorse
flows over the hills flushed at the seams
with orange broom. We agree to share botulism
if the crayfish roll at the tearooms
should fail us. Well yes. This is certainly
short enough to be happiness.
The morning's a ball
of silk unwound about us. You gather
it back with me at its centre.

Kennedy Park

(after a funeral)

those seconds   when the sky fills
with the black hail
        of sparrows
before they settle   at dark

a pale skein of sky   hanging
over us
the wind cutting closer
as we walk arm
                        in arm
under   skeletal   mid winter
trees

                        so much
for a fine delicate night   some several thousand
birds on the wing   pump   (little tissues skin feathers veins
as fine as blue thread)   fierce rhythms
they blot out the memory of the sun   their voices
are united   like our ancestors
it is our moment of common lament
crying in the dark horde
                        another parent
fell at noon
husband/lover   we are the grandparents now   the
   next in line
                        to die
what a cloud/what a crowded sky

heart   do you hear them stop   the quiet turning in on itself?

A prime minister gives presents
at a royal occasion

The short fat balding man bestows
china birds on royalty   the wife
is pretty is reported to pop gum
in private   her smile is bruised

but steady   they smile
             and smile
they have more china birds at
home   cutlery rattles   the small
round domed man eats   everyone

eats   the night beyond stirs
with eating   worms turn earth
moreporks regurgitate & spiders
track silverfish invade hymn

books in churches munching paper
like Moro bars   the couple take
the china birds holding them to
their breasts   ah aah thank you.

An aftermath

for J.M. Coetzee

The nightmare of the flood
had left the landscape pockmarked
and blue like the moon and then
the looting began and the man
wearing round spectacles made of smoke
coloured non-reflective
glass walked over the pitted
world with the woman with red
hair that would have shone in the sun
if there had been any left, shooting
the looters. Angry dogs, savage
and at loose, sprang at the couple
of the man with the shaded eyes handed
his pistol to the woman with red
hair, instructing her to shoot the animals.
When they came to me he handed
me the pistol and instructed
me to shoot the woman
in the stomach. The red strands and the blue
clay were mixed on the surface of the earth
and it was quite clearly my fault, though
it seemed I would be allowed
to go without questioning.

NEW POEMS

Queenslander Cottage

(for Janet Irwin)

1.

The wardrobes open to receive
my clothes. Tonight I'll lie down
in your bed while the pink light
glows
in the room beyond. I've been here
for years. I know you.

Well, this is not exactly true. I'm a stranger
in a borrowed house
and alone at evening
in another country
I absorb the assembled evidence:
>   pewter, rugs, books, globes
>   of glass brimming threads like spun
>   sugar, New Yorkers, music
>   Jane's pictures
>   on every wall, hints of the Hokianga —
a transplanted past, a relentless presence
in which I see myself reflected.

2.

It is morning:
from the stilt-legged verandah
I watch four crows advance
their voices gurgling
their steps mincing their eyes
staring hardly at mine. I look back, disturbed,
but not scared; the web of the house
draws me back. The first jacaranda blooms
heavy as a quilt, light as blue air
in the valley. I may never meet you

or, yes, it will happen. The history's as unshakeable
as this happiness, of knowing, and not knowing,
everything.

Being Friends

(for Jane L./ at a Japanese exhibition)

That
instant conspiracy
of delight

Miwa's ring form
clay silver
that massive warp of earth

and Tsuchiya's
Horizon line
an arc

of driftwood
        linked like fingers
man's abandoned (abandonment) material
re-formed (reformed), composed

pictures
painted
with persimmon juice

the broad Brisbane
River flowing

the afternoon
        waning
we resolve   more quickly
as we age

those we will trust   hours
at an exhibition
will do

Toby's Eggs

Toby wears his curls in a plait.
He picks the stone eggs from my bowl
on the hearth. This one malachite,
this rose quartz from Madagascar,
here rhodite, & that jade
from British Columbia, & another sandstone
from Kenya, & this one I bought
in a Parisian market,
& the one beside it is made of marble from Athens.
He places them, one by one,
against the eye's hollow, until his flesh
warms them.
Two-year-old Toby, mesmerized,
dismissing us from his presence.
Plump, buttery, black-eyed boy,
you're too young to travel alone. When you go
I will check the fit
of your shoes.

Writing home

I want to tell you
of the glittering water at Chania
where fishermen pull
nets by torchlight & about
wistaria in the streets
all this romantic *atmosphere*
            the way
    sun falls through slatted
blinds into the green
& white room
at the Doma
& so I will
& so I will
but first I'll tell
you about the girl squatting
amongst the red poppies
on the cliff while Elena
served fig preserve
at breakfast
& all that French family
at the next table
chortling, one by one,
then all together
at those innocent pearly buttocks
shining.

Scenes of the Land

The phone feels like
a telescope   I look straight
into her faraway

grown-up voice:
  a January day
109 railway wagons

roll over white
grass by an electric-
blue sea

somewhere near Opotiki
we think though thinking
back we're not sure
where we were a berry-

coloured child rides
her father's shoulders the train
on that horizon

click tschick click click tschick
        count the wagons darling
count count count

going on & on
while the blue-eyed Siamese called Oscar
that rode

everywhere with us never stopped
licking its fur
& its paws in the Fiat

I say: *hullo hullo are you there
how's life in the country?*

Black Hearts

(a scientist speaks of infecting New Zealand oak trees with truffle fungus)

In a cool chamber he extracts
the reverential salver
(a tupperware container)
the air is fraught
at the sight of three black
mounds such innuendo   we

speak of monstrous sows
driven to frenzies at the scent
tearing earth devouring
fingers of truffle gatherers
in their path (Colette said:
if I cannot eat too many

truffles I will not eat truffles
at all). They smell
        of vanilla
ice cream   how can I say
that it will not do? not here?
we can nurture these nuggets

with black marshmallow hearts
& gather them beneath leafy
branches but this   this is
        a moderate Presbyterian
land yet to learn profligacy   we
will drink Milo at bedtime.

Bulls provide semen for breeding programmes

From the way the bowler
  hatted men in the early
pictures gathered round
    at fairs watching, the eager
abashed boys in the background
    waiting for the chained live-in
lovers to mount in this
        controlled
            camp den
you'd think wouldn't you
that the semen would come gusting
out

    as if the creature were
an All Black or a champion
      fencer   somehow different
why else would they watch
those great shining beasts rubbing
    up to the steer's buttocks &
        ejaculating? but
it comes soundlessly as semen
    habitually does, a quick
shot into a hand-held plastic
    bag white thick and quite
        plentiful.

The Presence of M. at a School Reunion

'The lies we tell are part of the truth we live'
Michael Holroyd, biographer

If, out walking, we caught the scent
of penny royal in the air, or watched a twig
revolving in a circular eddy in the stream,
listened, perhaps, to the shush shush
shush of the trees in the gum belt,
that is not surprising. We know
how to watch, how to listen. We have always known.

But when we're dressed for roll call, like girls
aching for a party, M. turns
and says, recant. We shared this past. This
isn't the first time we've set off for school
together. How was it you came to see things
                    so differently
from me? What was I doing while you suffered
so much? We were both there.

Think on it.

The man who loved violets

M's mother reminds us of the vegetarian
neighbour who 'ate salads from one side of the plate
to the other covered with violets
and marigolds' and who 'so *loved*
violets *in particular* that he once
leaned down at a ball and ate
the fresh violet corsage from a girl's dress'.
We see him; ache with laughter. Imagine.
The cream breast. The dress (yellow,
perhaps, certainly chiffon). The small
blue-ish flowers trembling on the frail
stems amongst the green leaves. The flashing
white teeth set   in the pink gums.
Such crunching through a tango.

Prague Spring 1 (1968)

In an aquarium light
Karel sits in his restaurant
counting neon tetras and angel
fish. I still see the puzzled turn
of his head, the crease of his pale
broad face: 'It was cold
in the forest, their guns trained
on our backs all the time.' He
drinks to New Zealand. 'I went
under the wire, Palach
goes up in flames. This student,
this boy.' He lies
his head on his arms gasping
like a guppy.

Prague Spring 2 (1989)

A man on the president's balcony
wearing a black cloak or
a long heavy coat, you can't
always tell in those European
scenes of winter, faces the Vltava

River. He reads to the masses,
he reads them words. His words
have almost destroyed him, a playwright
in disguise. But listen, he speaks
without fear, his words will find

the right spot like a water diviner
with the twig alive in his hand,
water will rise to the surface,
the flames of Jan Palach's funeral pyre
will become reflections in a drop of rain.

A Woman Photographed

(text from Let Us Now Praise Famous Women*: Andrea Fisher)*

As she sleeps the arm head hair
of a woman fall
across the door
of her open-top
car. The image is highly sensuous;
we associate pleasure
with security:
  with knowing a Self
  however tenuous
or fleeting, and its relation
   to the Other.

Back and forth she carries us
across the fraught
and endless narratives *who*
is she, what is she doing?

  is it
me, is it her? Her

absent body
is replaced
by the car. Horizontal strokes of light
      and shadow
alternate over her arm and onto
the paralleling curves. Through
the extension of softly
lit surfaces it may be thought
that face arm and car
become
her one
continuous
  skin.

Carole Something Like a Lombard

Carole Lombard: 'One of Hollywood's most popular blondes, a kind of freewheeling sophisticated Jean Harlow; good at everything from sensitive drama to screwball comedy.'
Illustrated Directory of Film Stars, *Quinlan, 1981*

(Lombard died in a plane crash over the Atlantic in 1942.)

There is a beginning, a middle &
an end, I say,
you can't avoid these factors even
in the most experimental
form *they exist*. The story
of course can be *long*
or short, there are *no*
absolutes, no rules you
can lay down for how to say
what you must, though it is
              useful —
I say —
to know the rules so that you understand
what it is that you are breaking

Carole   friend
named in fact after that silvery cataclysmic blonde
who took such an unruly unexpected plunge
into a warring sea

so you   too   taking
to the indecipherable dark
a car leaping on its side
landing   at the water's edge

blind windows of the Pines Cabaret peering down
              in the storm
it would be helpful to this story

to avoid death, it's been done before, the symmetry
of self-fulfilling prophecy's too perfect,
it would have been convenient
if you could have stayed
and told your own story

which you almost did   I expect
to die
you sd
at yr funeral service the tape
rescued from an archive   I don't
want any funeral service I conduct turned into a 2ZM
roadshow this is not talkback the officiating
minister sd but yes
I sd

it is, she's still got something to say, while you
explained on the crackling speaker
that it had been hard your life gone astray
bits mislaid but you knew where
you were coming from   &
where you were going. (Though
this hadn't been planned this
accidental occurrence crawling on hands
& knees across the sand
to your child you sd are you
all right will you be all right now before the fairy-
tale closing)
        but the tape ran out didn't tell
        it all   the varieties & nature of despair
        or just what it was like when you were laughing.

In the mail a picture arrives
after a decade
or so   Carole silvery blonde and cataclysmic
& ordinary
as ever   younger than I knew her   in twinset
& pearls   with a baby
in her lap   it's easy

to look in the mirror ask
which of us survived our stance
   at least   interchangeable before various
crashes   which one

endures you could say like
Lazarus I walked again but something like a Lombard   she's sitting
on the kitchen table *framed*

in black and white   but that's
too easy the story is, after all, too good
to be true, too bad for anyone
to make up.

Wakeful Nights

1

In the beginning they were rare
enough, hot summer nights
up north under a low farm
                              ceiling,
the stinging contraction
of an iron roof   the bawdy reek
of plums at the window
                              pane

and a morepork crying
                  go *now*
go *now* at 3 a.m.
until, as if a sleepwalker, I
padded on silent feet
over paddocks to the river's
edge and a fallen poplar

slung above North River;
                           listening
from its branches I heard
the dark water swirl round matted
willow roots & God's voice
saying it will always be
                           too *late*
too *late* to tell it all.

2

Rotorua November
Nineteen fifty seven: I
strung a Guy Fawke's effigy

from the archway to Government
Gardens, clattering on
needlepoint heels on the tar, how

wild the night how pleasant
the waxed begonias in
their beds: afterwards lying

awake for weeks waiting
for the police.   I did
that with boys, for their square

fingernails their intricate
wiry curls   the backs of
their cars the blind butting

of their tongues. They were
generous, they gave me
sleeplessness
            and trouble.

3

Leigh, North Auckland the Jolly
Fisherman's Lodge, approached
from the wharves over slatted
wooden bridges,   suitcases
in hand.   Your letter arrived
for my birthday 1960:
'surprise surprise two letters
from me and none from you, send
me a telegram when you
decide.' All I did was read

all week watching the spinifex
turn over on the sand. Only
when the distant lights of boats shone
through the shadow of the navy

sea burning beyond the granite
cliffs, the haunted clay,
was it cool enough to consider
your proposal;
                    in the end
I said yes, a strange
place to choose a life.

4

In the dark the children's faces
like magnolia flowers on the pillows.
Whose turn to chase the milkman's
night delivery down the frosty road
the forgotten bottles clanking
against our dressing gowns? Those
children drank 8 pints a day.

5

These wakeful nights went hand
in hand with grit, mad laughter
and tears; they were bodies turning
left to right right to left
against the gaunt, the red-eyed
dream. We listened to the winds
that sweep across
            Te Whanganui a Tara,
their muttered *kiss gasp kiss*
at the window pane, as we sought
each other's bones.   Instead
of resting, we tore the blankets
from side to side, avenging
late parties, nightmares, ordinary deceits.
Oh, in the end, we said
                        enough.

6

As the last light star
dissolves above the sea, you
place the white cup beside
the bed, love so various
has become kind: 'how did
            you sleep?' the ritual
enquiry;
                  'not badly'
I tell you,
      remembering
   one thought leading
to the next as the Judas
sheep leads its brothers up
the slaughterhouse ramp and
slips away, words ever
treacherous; the notebooks
go on filling night
            by lighted night,
those hours at last are friends.

   Do not think me changed, my
fabled fault and virtue to
love persistently, nothing
changes that.   I have simply
learned to guard the word
beyond the powerful dark;
            the sun fans along the hill
tops, I watch the bay, the sky
the heavy heavy languor
of the green curtain lifting.

The Yellow Beak

(for Ian)

The River Kwai continued strange and wonderful,
a place where land crabs scuttled,
snakes slid near the jungle tracks,
and waterfalls leapt through the mountain passes.
At nights the tunnel walls that linked
the hotel moved with a dark lace
of lizards, a leopard-like fishing
cat arched its back, caged
and dangerous, near the entrance
to the compound, and the air
conditioning rattled like hail storms.

In the afternoons as we rested, a hornbill,
knee-high and tame, stretched
its wings over and again
beside us, and when we tired
of admiring it, took my foot,
altogether encompassing the shoe
in the chrome-yellow scythe of its beak.

But on the last day, near where we sat,
a mad dog rushed out
of the trees, swift and shocking,
to attack the hornbill,
going at its bright beak. The bird's handler,
defending it, was torn by the dog,
while another man, mysterious and silent-
footed, with shrouded mouth, appeared and,
with a machine gun, shot the dog *ra-ta-tat tat*.

We saw, then, the man,
his bird with the terrible meat-stump
of its face, and the dead dog
in a plastic bag, loaded

on a jeep and driven
away. 'Rabies tests,'
someone muttered, grim-faced.

The menacing man with the gun
melted back into the hotel
shadows to wait for other
bandits. But what will happen
to the bird? we asked at the desk. They smiled
orientally, wanting
        us to go away happy.
It will grow a new beak, they said.

OTHER NEW ZEALAND TITLES
AVAILABLE IN VINTAGE EDITIONS

Strained Relations by Gaelyn Gordon
Holy Terrors and Other Stories by Amelia Batistich
The Peace Monster by John Smythe
Always the Islands of Memory by Noel Virtue*
To the Is-land by Janet Frame*
An Angel At My Table by Janet Frame*
A Population of One by Alice Glenday
Strangers in Paradise by Jonathan Eisen and
Katherine Joyce Smith
Man With Two Arms and Other Stories
by Norman Bilbrough
Finding Out by Elspeth Sandys**

* Available only in New Zealand
** Available only in New Zealand and Australia